RAIN AND GRAVESTONES

by

John Swain

Rain and Gravestones

© 2013 by John Swain

Published 1 September 2013

as Crisis Chronicles #45

Cover photo © 2013 by John Swain

ISBN-13: 978-0615873404

Crisis Chronicles Press

3344 W. 105th Street #4

Cleveland, Ohio 44111 USA

http://press.crisischronicles.com &

facebook.com/crisischroniclespress

John Burroughs, editor/publisher

email: jc@crisischronicles.com

Table of Contents

Acknowledgments

Bigger Stones, Bone Orchard, Camel Saloon, A Clean, Well-Lighted Place, Dark Chaos, Eunoia Review, Flutter, Full of Crow, Green Panda Press, Mad Rush, Phantom Kangaroo, Pipe Dream, PressBoardPress, Rainbow Rose, Red Fez, Red Poppy, Rufous Salon, Rusty Nail, Sparkbright, Up the Staircase, and Yes Poetry.

At the Ceiling

Moon of lights
on the dark walk
in the tall grass.
A girl in furs
with black flowers
in blonde hair.
I secured balance
in tree movement,
stars dripping.
The dogs bay
in rage at silence
and a trespass
into the fearing.
I struck with fist
at the ceiling
of this red dirt.

The Black Hours

The pages in black tint
writ with silver scripts
and the blue gold inlay.
I saw the crossed man
hanging from the wire
in passion surrendered.
The night and the seas
exchanged a cremation
the poets interpret.
I read the black hours
like a haunted passage
I am confined to relive.
The beauty of the work
contains its destruction
like rain inks on glass.

With His Weapon

Each with his weapon
kept the waters beyond
the outside gate.
I remain unfortunate
to have ever believed
in you and God
and God in you or me.
I must rid myself
of the impulse
toward love's ambition numbed
in its sabotage.
Sun left the edges of your body
tied close to the sea
on a bed of sand
like the embers of trees
rest in the cooling.

Fore Edge of a Precious Book

One leaf reflects sun gilding the hill
like the fore edge of a precious book opens,
rain scent clings to autumn ground.
The lake reaches for you through blue trees
and I chased as land repositions the grave,
I could not cry through your laughter.
Rust from the iron gate fell like a petal
as you crossed the arching threshold
away from me and into the world like a child.
Then we were alone with ourselves
each to a mutual dream arising like sails
far on the water where the light touches.

The Jasmine

Night aromatic upon the jasmine
presages relief from the distrust
spread by the well,
I took money to the park square.
Banyans glow holding the moon
like a white apple
in the dream written upon a wick
soon to be burned in forgetting.
I tired of the welt and the insects
in the stillness of gate and alley,
I stepped over a blue wall laying
torn like evening dress in coffin.
Coolness of stones in the garden
against the forehead
and cup of porcelain
I accepted in rest and inheritance.

Beneath the Lighthouse

In the shallows
beneath the lighthouse,
a boy drowned
where we swam
and climbed
toward the sun
upon a pillar of rocks
the day before.
I hear his voice
in a white sail raising
far on the lake
and the osprey
touching water
for a silver fish.
Angels serrate
the edges of the map
I drew on my hand
as I grazed
the expanse of waves
like his shoulder
to remember
a wild innocence.

Oak Moss

Stone bath
and fountain
spring dug
on the ridge
of oak moss
and trace.
I stripped the branches
with knife
and hand
for leaves
to hide
the anxiety
of returning
to hell
for each pomegranate.
I stepped into
the dry pool
for a woman
living at once
in a song
and painting.

Burnt Church

Through the oaks
stood the ruins
of a burnt church.
I took black sand
through my fingers
and inhaled
perfumes of char.
Light in arches
met their shadows
in eclipsing kiss.
A new tree began
in the empty turret
like a pennon.
I dragged myself
off of the ground
on broken chains.

The Cruse

Red dragonflies sparkled
when she poured water
from the cruse onto a rag
for the back of my neck.
I dreamed of the strength
to recover
and live simply and clean
for the sake of her favor.
I cooled under the sheets
in the air
as she counted out beads.
The window kept the day
alive for us
until a sleep finally came
and I turned from her face.

Fire Once Lived

I slipped behind
the outcropping
like a black door.
The cavern moved
in the dark shape
of whales diving
to grave or birth.
In the entrance
like a familiar bed
I lay where a fire
once lived, still
each taken breath
charred my lungs
and nostrils.
Confined to become
my own guidance
without a passage
of safety,
I spread the ash
in an image book.

Cupbearer

The cover morn
lifts in a light
the shape of prey
afeared to sleep
through the kill.
I am learning
to only serve you
with my life
like a cupbearer
sips for poison
with a loyalty
never questioned.
Birds strayed
beyond sky gates
like the pool
of a fountain
where I drew water
for your bathing.

Crush of a Mountain

An undeserved comfort
like a sheet
to lay on the bed
then the air.
The day pressed my bones
into powder
for a husk
keeping the seed
grown on earth.
Leave me
and let
the crush of a mountain
raise me
on stones of sky
to the light of birds.
I have seen many eagles
and here I would like to fall
on the claim
like the breath God said.

Sky Lanterns

Tonight we lit
sky lanterns
in the empty field
behind the house.
The candle fire
black as crows
hanging jagged
in the air
rattling trees.
I tried to describe
the spectra
of competing
and simultaneous
living energies,
though the line
I carved on bark
remained an apparition.
A bitter herb
flavored the water
in the bowl
earth offered
to our mouths.

Effigy of the Giving

Parting before autumn
a kingfisher came
like a sorcerer
from the blue fire
of the bay.
I ate the pomegranates
and kept the seeds
preserved inside me
to mourn
for the corn's daughter.
The field bares stones
to raise an effigy
of the giving
and of our aspirations
shattered like a harrow.

Plain Stone

Thaw from the creek rocks made a quiet rain,
I searched for artifacts in the pools and grass,
but could not find a relic touched with power.
I will build a stable dwelling again in myself
with plain stone for which no one found a use,
a ghost inside the sunlight provided me with hours.
And the efforts in solitude hang upon nothing
like the world made of our bodies and trees.
I tried to unsew my lips enough to please you.
The dripping water cleansed my hands of earth
as the sky captured itself in amber beyond the ridge,
then I walked into the open with eyes of praise.

Dune Lavender Clematis

Sunset on dune lavender clematis
though oats stayed gold for the crow
and the people refusing to speak
upon greeting,
I hated their faces in my weakness.
Water dripping
from the balcony stained the page
torn from an antique history book
I found earlier on the sand.
I traced the image of the terebinth
on my palms pressing the weather
for a hidden burial.
Dark ink blurred like another night
when I went outside
to the eyeless sea reading psalters,
I archived the bruit of the shallow.

Hibiscus Tea

Field became another sky
when snow fell
over the first winter night.
In the drift on the hill
we warmed beneath my coat
and sipped hibiscus tea
from a silver bowl I carried.
Trees floated from the ice
as she polished a rabbit jaw
and dropped prayer beads
to mark our path.
Fear darkened my heart
so I kneeled on my teeth
gone away to rejoicing her.

Venture

Winter blue sky inviolate.
Cold water on limestones
in a valley of dead leaves
the color of whiskey.
Cranes, crows, and hawk
unveiled the air
for the play of my breath.
I cut my hand on a fence
and then loved
what openness becomes.
The creek found the lake
like its destiny
as I moved to the ending
forgetful of reasons.
Sweetness of the hickory
accompanies the venture
to map the chasm
grown in blue reflection.

Flint

The ember after
the flint against
the steel for fire
as I held a glass
to capture smoke
above a bowl
of fragrant sap.
The room is new
for the funeral
of several days
laying on the bed
like a scroll
of hieroglyphics.
I bit my tongue
to sing ghazals
and long for the only
body of prayer
to bury the weight
of sun over me.

Tinder

Grasses at the stream
provide a tinder to lie
and now I am numb
to the barking
and the mountain.
A child girl whispered
into a deer skull
while I brought gifts
of tea and red silk
from the other land
I traveled by myself.
I mended the liveries
without obligation
or self-impetus
before the discipline
we turned into an art.

Rain and Gravestones

Then red trees turned barer by each afternoon
like a bruise disappears and mice empty the silos,
vermin also enter the libraries gnawing on books.
I drove the road under shadows of the dying corn
to the rain and family gravestones.
Our faith was tried by ordeal of water
as I wore the same clothing and bones
afraid for the woman and girl who come visit me.
And the mulled wine and apples colored the sky
like them I am widowed and childless.
I rubbed the epitaphs to make a name for myself
when the chapel owl took flight like a giant moth.

In the Sand

Tables of waves
in the night
like commandment.
I dove
in all my clothes
soon lost
to the ocean
and that was youth.
The dunes knew
many bodies
and we had our time
to hide alone
in vinous mouths.
I always wear
the white flower
pressed between
your shoulders
in the sand
to inspire
like a holy book.

Coracle

Sea green sun warmed
the pathway toward
an argus noon.
I watched the ospreys
circle and dive
into my swimming.
I read the telling
of the unnoticed
and was shown opening.
The wind inscribed
its voice on the reeds
like a coracle to leave
the place I wanted to stay
remaining a stranger
cast from the people.
Light painted my craft
so fragile
like a ship on the sea.

Torch

River field
of fireflies
mingled
with yellow
green stars.
I looked at you
like a deer
and raised
your legs
around my waist
in flight
and stillness.
Darkening
again
the sky became
a tree shadow
I feared
like a person
until you formed
a shared torch.

As Only Sleep

Intimate as only sleep,
the candle and a cross
like a story torn.
And darkened like rain
the glimpse of her face
brought me nothingness
like the peace
of which I dreamed.
I stitched Xs for death
on my tongue and wrist
to be finally real
like a man in strength.
The hallway leaned to lead
away to the world
I had shattered to find.

Goats

After the goats
wandered the forest
in the moon pooled
all luminous
on the sick girl,
I scraped her neck
with a dog fang
and dusted her face
with clay powder.
Then her spirit
turned
like a cure
and I drove a peg
into the ground.
She only came back
to go away.

John Swain lives in Louisville, Kentucky. He is the author of the following chapbooks: *Prominences* and *Sinking of the Cloth* [Flutter Press]; *Set Apart Before the World Was Made* [Calliope Nerve Media]; *Burnt Palmistry* [Full of Crow]; *Handing the Cask* [erbacce press]; *Fragments of Calendars* [Thunderclap Press]; and *White Vases* [Crisis Chronicles Press].